A THOUSAND REASONS
FOR LIVING

A THOUSAND REASONS
FOR LIVING

Dom Helder Camara

Edited by José de Broucker

Translated by Alan Neame

FORTRESS PRESS   PHILADELPHIA

Originally published in French as *Mille raisons pour vivre*
by Editions du Seuil, 27 rue Jacob, Paris VIe.

English translation copyright © 1981
by Darton, Longman and Todd

Library of Congress Cataloging in Publication Data

Câmara, Hélder, 1909 –
  A thousand reasons for living.

  Translation of: Mille raisons pour vivre.
  1. Meditations. I. Broucker, José de. II. Title.
BX2186.C21813 1981   242   81-43070
ISBN 0-8006-0664-7   AACR2

9003E81   Printed in the United States of America   1–664

CONTENTS

INTRODUCTION

The first time I went travelling with Dom Helder
Camara, I was in for a surprise. We happened to
be passing a field with some cows in it. One of the
cows raised its head to look at us. Dom Helder
acknowledged its interest with a little wave.

Later on, with the same little wave and a smile
in his eyes, he passed the time of day with a little
white cloud which was idling in the sun, with a
jet aircraft glittering high in the sky, with a
church-bell which happened to be ringing as we
went through the village, with a little boy hopping
home from school with his satchel on his back,
with a rabbit running across the road and with a
flower which, when we drew up, was waiting for
him as he got out of the car.

I realized, that day, that the little Archbishop of
Recife's unrelenting struggle for men really to be
able to live together as brothers had its roots in an
intimate communion with the entire creation. For
him, there is no creature that does not bear the
Creator's living and evident mark on it.

The way Dom Helder spends his days is no

mystery. They are completely available to others, to all and sundry, great and small, by appointment or unannounced. His listens, he advises. He listens, he gives a decision. He listens, he helps. Unfailingly present, available, attentive.

By day, Dom Helder unstintingly distributes what he has received during the night.

Ever since he was at his seminary, it has been his habit to get up in the small hours, at about two o'clock. In the silent darkness, he listens, listens all the time. Then it is he hears the voices that daytime noises tend to drown. God talks to him, nature too, and the human heart. All the previous day's and coming day's encounters fall into place and proportion for the Offertory, Consecration and Communion. Holy Mass then works the transformation of prayer into life and of life into prayer. Day dives into darkness to re-emerge from it like a baptism constantly renewed.

During his nightly vigils, Dom Helder Camara writes. Letters, reports, speeches. Meditations too: these he calls 'Father Joseph's Meditations', in honour of his inseparable Guardian Angel.

The meditations are not poems. Dom Helder attaches no literary value or ambition to them. He regards them more like wild flowers, fading as soon as open. That they have been preserved at all is due only to his spiritual director's orders, given years ago now, and to the care and attention of loyal friends.

The thousands and thousands of meditations,

written night after night over a period of some fifty years, constitute a book of Wisdom, a hymn to the creation, a collection of Fioretti, and a Mass for the world, all combined.

In making this anthology, the contents of which are arranged in chronological order, I have principally drawn on a selection made in Rio by some of Dom Helder's friends, notably the great writer and critic Alceu Amoroso Lima, and published by Civilização Brasileira under the title *Mil Razões para viver* (A Thousand Reasons for Living).

The meditations chosen for this book are introduced by three prose pieces in the same vein: three of Dom Helder's daily radio-talks broadcast on Radio-Olinda.

I should like to thank Charles Antoine for the help he has given me in preparing this book for the press.

JOSÉ DE BROUCKER

CHILDREN WILL GET THE POINT . . .

In the full bus, packed to overflowing actually, everyone's attention was drawn to a small boy holding a scrap of wood with extreme care. One lady couldn't bear it any longer and asked him why he was being so careful about this worthless scrap of wood.

He explained, 'I am taking a little ant for a ride. She's my great friend. It's her first trip in a bus.'

Who would ever have thought the kid could have so much poetry and kindness in him!

I couldn't keep my eyes off him. When he got off the bus, I got off too. I felt that here was someone I could really talk to.

I explained that I too was very fond of little ants. And I told him about the only time when the ants and I had ever been at cross-purposes.

One night, our little ants at home gobbled up our rosebush. Next morning, I caught Sonja, a little red lady-ant and one of the cleverest I ever met in my life. I didn't squeeze her angrily—for God preserve me from anger! But I did hold her with a certain firmness. Her little foot was trembling and her heart was beating fit to burst.

I asked her why they had gobbled up my rosebush in a single night.

Miss Sonja replied, 'Do you think you're the only person to like roses?'

At first I was taken aback, but then retorted, 'Eating seems a funny way of loving!'

At which Sonja nearly made me die of shame by asking, 'Isn't that what you do at Holy Communion?'

I apologized to her and set her free, carefully putting her back on the ground.

For the next three days, all the ants looked at me askance.

Unable to bear this any longer, I called Sonja and asked her to help me.

And this is how, by means of Sonja, I taught the ants to smell the roses instead of eating them. I explained to them that kissing roses goes on all over the place. But not up here in Nordeste—we just smell them.

I invited the little boy who was taking his ant-friend for a bus-ride to come and visit our garden one moonlit night, and see all the ants climbing up the rosebush and smelling the roses.

The child didn't react like a grown-up: he wasn't surprised, he didn't disbelieve me. He thought it was great!

So I then told him how, one day, I met a young ant called Claudia, who was limping. We were in the garden at home. With her permission, I turned her over on her back to see what was the matter with her tiny foot.

So it was that Claudia for the first time saw the sky—for ants are just like us—go, go, go, run, run, run, never pausing to look up and gaze at the sky!

On seeing the sky for the first time, Claudia lay open-mouthed with amazement and delight. I soon realized there was no point in asking her about her foot. She wasn't listening. She was looking at the sky.

I told the little boy as he got into another bus carrying his ant on the bit of wood, 'If you come to my house one moonlight night, you may very well find the little ants lying on their backs with their heads in the grass, gazing at the moon.'

Grown-ups, important people, forgive me if I have disappointed or shocked you by forgetting about you for a moment and talking to the children. Didn't Christ say that you can't go to heaven unless you become like little children?

GROWN-UPS JUST DON'T UNDERSTAND

The kid's mother was firmly convinced that he had
lost the house-key. So she made him turn out both
his trouser pockets and both the pockets in his
jacket.

What didn't come out! Everything, except the
key.

This made the boy's mother angrier than ever.
As far as she could see, the odds and ends with
which his pockets were stuffed were nothing but
trash. How hard it is to understand children!

How nostalgic I feel for my childhood pockets!
They were just the same!

An empty cotton-reel! Could Mother ever grasp
the fact that what looked like a cotton-reel was
really a radio-telephone to be used when crossing
deserts?

A piece of string! How could a grown-up ever
agree that it wasn't a piece of string at all but a
magic tightrope for stretching from mountain to
mountain, or over the water for crossing torrents
in spate?

Pebbles of all shapes and colours: that really did

make grown-ups frown, since it was quite beyond them to believe that these were fragments of moon-rock brought back by an astronaut!

The kid's mother watched the most unlikely and unexpected things coming out of his pockets, all but the house-key. When a little bell appeared, she exploded, 'At last, that's something I do understand. A little bell! You deserve to have one tied round your neck, round your wrists and round your ankles, you clown!'

The little boy looked very sad at this but said nothing. I was dying to intervene and say, 'But can't you see? It's a magic bell brought by a fish from the bottom of the sea! Can't you see, it's a bell for frightening sadness away and summoning joy?' That's what I wanted to say, but I kept quiet. She wouldn't have understood. Grown-ups find it so hard to understand the simplest of things.

Out of the child's pockets, I recall, also came some seeds, a nail, a top, a scrap of cloth, a photo of Bob Dylan . . .

The scrap of cloth—what could be more obvious?—was the tail of a kite. The top was presumably the champion dancer of all the tops in the world. The seeds, with a little creative imagination, might give birth to anything one pleased.

The nail! Well, the nail . . . but why this mania for wanting an explanation for everything? Why not think of the nail as a surprise? Before tonight, you see if it hasn't been put to good use half a dozen times!

As for the photo of Bob Dylan, it really would be the end if you were to ask what that is for!

How patient children have to be when dealing with grown-ups!

GOD'S FOOL

Out in the open, near my home, sleeps one of God's fools, a wonderful little madman.

I often had a chat with him. I asked him if he hadn't got anywhere to sleep. Astonished at my question, he replied, 'Of course I have! There's no shortage of earth, no shortage of sky!'

I persisted in my logical way. 'But what about when it rains?' To which he, as quick as you please: 'Do you think I never take a shower?'

I asked him whether he was hungry, whether he would like something to eat. 'What I like is singing. Will you listen? I was born to sing.' How could I resist? I asked him to sing.

To a folk-tune popular in our Nordeste, he sang something like this:

Proud Sirs, tell me please,
   Tell me please, will ye:
Are you going to die? If yes,
Pride is not your worst disease,
   It's being plain silly!

And before I could laugh or applaud, he was

roaring with laughter and clapping his hands as though the singer had been someone else.

I insisted on offering him some food, reminding him that, though a bird certainly sings, it eats too.

This time, I managed to convince him. I went and fetched him a little food in a billy-can. He laughed at my stupidity. 'I want a guava! Little birds eat guavas!'

I still haven't managed to find out what his name is. Whenever I ask him, he gives me a different answer: 'You can call me Blackbird' . . . 'Call me Grouse, that's all right too' . . . 'I know I'm not Canary.'

I like it when he sings without knowing anyone is listening:

Linnet, O Linnet,
Don't try and make money,
   For money's like glue
And once you are in it,
   No flying for you!

I asked him one day if he said his prayers. He found my question hard to understand. All he could say was:

Children throw stones at me,
   I fly, I laugh, I sing!

At one point I thought of having him put in an asylum, where some doctor friends of mine might have been able to find out what was wrong with him and perhaps make him better.

14

But I quickly realized that he and we should all be losers by the change.

There are all too many people with their rational and ultra-rational heads properly screwed on. Perhaps that is why we keep misunderstanding one another and why the world is in such confusion . . .

Keep on the wing, Fool of God, perhaps Blackbird, possibly Grouse, but not Canary!

Go on singing, go on singing. I shall do my best to treasure God's wisdom speaking through your madness. And whenever I can, I shall put a ripe guava aside for you, preferably one already pecked by some little bird, your brother!

MEDITATIONS

I wish I were
a humble puddle
that would reflect the sky!

20 April 1947

How long, my God—
mankind and sea
are we to waver
between flood
and ebb?

4 January 1951

To cling to the earth,
to anchor yourself to the ground
by all the roots you have,
is more than your mere right,
it is your life,
your instinct,
your reason for existing.
Man, however
—forgive me!—
is something rather more
than a mere tree.

25 March 1951

A mystery confounding human reason:
life feeds on death.
In the Eucharist alone,
life feeds on life.

28 March 1951

'What a lot of shells wasted
on this lonely beach!
They would bring happiness
to thousands of children . . .'

He didn't understand
that the waves, the sea's daughters,
are lovely children who
love playing with shells too.

9 April 1951

Man stretches telephone wires
all across the city,
not content
until he's got
the whole world within earshot.

The radio,
not needing wires at all,
incites and excites the chatterbox even more.
Where are our inventors?
We urgently need inventions
as aids to silence,
to protect it,
save it.

27 April 1951

All, absolutely all,
by your grace
speaks to me of You.

When I write
I ask
in your hands to be
the blank sheet of paper
where You can write what You please.

When I skim through a book
I feel acutely anxious
that such a lot of words should not go fruitless
and that no one should write
without some happy message for the world.

Every step I take
reminds me
that, wherever I am going,
I am always on the march to eternity.

The din of human life,
the dry leaves eddying on the ground,
the passing cars,
shop-windows full of goods,
the policeman on point-duty,

the milk-float,
the poor man begging,
the staircase and the lift,
the railway lines, the furrows of the sea,
the pedigree dog and the ownerless dog,
the pregnant woman,
the paper-boy,
the man who sweeps the streets,
the church, the school,
the office and the factory,
streets being widened,
hills being laid low,
the outward and the homeward road,
the key I use to open my front door;
whether sleeping or waking—
all, all, all
makes me think of You.

What can I give to the Lord
for all He has given to me?

5 May 1951

'Prodigal son who art in heaven:

Son who saved yourself by trusting,
serving since as an example
to millions of prodigals,
son who knew the horror of absence,
the emptiness of sin
and yearning for his father's house,
help me to pray, this agonizing night,
for prodigal parents
whose sin consists
in turning Christ's parable upside down
by erasing the Father's image in themselves.

15 May 1951

The excise-men are blind, so blind . . .

When I approach
customs officials
or the police,
I smile, happy
because no one can discover
the divine contraband
I carry with me,
that invisible passenger
whose very discreet presence
only the eyes of angels
can detect.

28 October 1951

28

Meditation for the machine age

Floor after floor,
tenth, eleventh, twelfth, thirteenth, fourteenth,
and I pray softly, inside me,
'Snatch us out of the ephemeral!
Lift us up to You!
Do not let us take root
in the world of man.'

Floor after floor,
sixteenth, fifteenth, fourteenth, thirteenth,
and in thought I pray,
'You who came down from heaven,
You who became incarnate,
teach me to come down
but not demean myself!'

11 February 1952

Leave your cares on the threshold of sleep.

Leave your worries,
all bitterness,
all rancour,
or you will feel as weary
as if you had slept
fully dressed, with your boots and your hat on.

19 September 1952

A word in season

Do not make God
your pillow,
or prayer
your eiderdown.

4 January 1953

If only people grasped the point
that the true fourth dimension
is the vision of the invisible
and the prospect of eternity!

20 January 1953

Cardiac arrhythmia, help me to think

in broken cadence,
loss of balance,
uncontrolled gestures,
countless stammerings . . .

21 January 1953

On the bare wall
was left a single nail
for a picture which had gone.
Are more needed
to prompt me to pray,
when three nails supported
the Redeemer of the world?

11 November 1953

You will be very poor
all the while you don't discover:
it's not with your eyes open
that you see the clearest.

You will be very naive
all the while you don't find out:
with your lips closed
you can have silences
far richer
than a spate of words.

You will be very clumsy
all the while you don't see:
with your hands joined
you can have more effect
than by moving them about,
which, without meaning to,
can wound.

14 December 1953

I was going to complain about the taxi-driver
who had flagged up: FREE
but would not serve me
when it struck me
that we cut an even worse figure
—and who is exempt?—
with our pretentious slogan:
FREEDOM

2 May 1954

Blocks of concrete, bless ye the Lord!

I was afraid
that with their blocks of concrete
the skyscrapers might wound the
dawn.

But you ought to see
how sensitive they are
to the morning light,
how they disarm
and lose their cutting edge
and steely soul!

They too are caught
in the irresistible spell
of the holy hour
when the whole natural world
in rapture chants
creation's hymn of praise.

22 August 1954

What will you say?

Look about you:
from the stars in their millions
in the heights,
to the stones, the water,
to the animals and plants,
you walk
among voiceless beings.
Look about you again:
look
until you see the invisible,
and you will tremble
at the silence of the angels
and the silence of God.

Speak, then . . .

10 October 1954

Eyes to see and ears to hear

Always spare a glance
of brotherly fellow-feeling
for tiny little stations
where the great expresses
hardly ever stop.
Haven't they something to tell you?
Don't they remind you of someone?

15 October 1954

Pilgrim:
when your ship,
long moored in harbour,
gives you the illusion
of being a house;
when your ship
begins to put down roots
in the stagnant water by the quay:
put out to sea!
Save your boat's journeying soul
and your own pilgrim soul,
cost what it may.

27 October 1954

40

Food for thought

The child was having a fine old time
at the open piano,
striking any old note
just for the pleasure of making a din,
just for the fun of producing sounds,
and not in the least concerned
about music in any sense,
exactly as we, so often,
have a fine old time with love.

18 December 1954

When hard work
soaks the shirts of humble folk,
look about you and you'll see
angels gathering
drops of sweat
as though gathering diamonds.

12 January 1955

Between being shade,
giving shade
and casting shade
lie gulfs
over which
God alone
can guide us.

16 January 1955

Don't get cross about the echo

Rather, give thanks
if everything on earth
pulsates within your breast,
transformed to prayer or song.

11 February 1955

44

Try
and put your hand
through the double-glazing,
and you will know the horror
of being beside the beloved
and feeling the double barrier
of egoism between you.

14 March 1955

Expecting to be deprived of his portfolio,
the minister
has the drawers tidied,
documents shredded,
the whole place put in order.

What a warning to ephemeral creatures
under constant threat
of being deprived of more than a ministry:
of life!

1 April 1955

I opened the child's exercise-book

All the problems solved.
Full marks.
Oh, if life
were as simple as that!

2 April 1955

Excessive profit-seeking

If the sun were as thirsty
and greedy as you,
not one puddle of water,
not one drop of dew,
would be left on the face of the earth.

19 April 1955

If you button a button
in a button-hole not the right one
it then becomes impossible
to button up the other ones right.

9 August 1955

In praise of varnish.

If it gives a shine to what is new,
it emphasizes what in fact is true.
If it gives a shine to what is old,
why then
it merits more respect than ever,
like the transfiguring smile
on the faces of happy old people
who understand how to grow old.

26 September 1955

Do you think land has no feelings?

I saw a building-plot
die of shame
at being put up for sale
like a slave
with a price
tied round his neck.

30 November 1955

I love flowers more and more

They speak to me
of how ephemeral life is
and make me face up
to eternity.

11 July 1956

I love looking at you,
hundred-year-old tree,
loaded with shoots and boughs
as though you were a stripling.
Teach me the secret
of growing old like you,
open to life, to youth, to dreams,
as somebody aware
that youth and age
are merely steps
towards eternity.

9 July 1957

Of all your lessons, Master,
one is so important
I forget about the rest . . .

Teach me to reach for the infinite,
the light, which on the horizon,
helps heaven come down to earth
and earth rise up to heaven.

12 July 1957

Don't tell me you don't know . . .

Fisherman skilled in watery matters,
how many fathoms of line
do I need
to plumb the human heart?
How can it be the human heart
is as deep as any sea?

16 February 1959

I like the sort of birds
that fall in love with stars
and drop, worn out
from trying to catch
their light.

19 February 1959

The unattainable ideal

Who will grant me
to be as loyal, discreet and silent
as my shadow is!

5 March 1959

Be careful, road-sweeper . . .

I've noticed how carefully you put aside
anything
that may still have some value.
Have you, while sweeping, ever come across
ruined fortunes,
fallen empires,
shreds of glory? . . .
Road-sweeper, show some respect
if any old bits of dreams,
life,
love,
turn up . . .

8 March 1959

Do not condemn us
to be alone
when together.
Allow us
to be together
when alone.

4 May 1959

Tomorrow, possibly . . .

One day,
for each of us,
the sun will rise
for the last time.
Light, my sister,
can there not be some way
of warning me
that my last day has come?
But still
the gospel precept
is the best:
to live each day
as if my last
or, better still,
as if always
my first.

8 May 1959

I don't want white lines
down the middle of my streets.

My streets
like my highways
have no edges,
just as they have
no beginning
or end.

29 December 1959

For the love of God, answer me!

Where are you, children,
to tell me about your toys,
poets
to tell me about your dreams,
madmen
to tell me about your frenzies,
sick people
to tell me about your sufferings,
the happy, the unhappy,
the saints and the sinners,
the young and the aged,
the dead and the living,
believers, unbelievers,
men and angels,
animals and plants,
all you creatures
of all worlds?

Wretched me,
if I were to go
up to God's altar alone!

22 February 1960

By the grace You grant me
of silence without loneliness,
give me the right to plead,
to clamour
for my brothers
imprisoned in
a loneliness without silence!

4 March 1960

The little old woman said to me,
oddly,
on receiving my alms,
'God be with you
in the hours of the cold sweats!'
The plural seemed odd:
I could only think of death.
Unhesitating,
she replied,
'You don't die only once.
Each time your sweat comes cold
—illness, fear, hope, shock—
then only God can help you.'

8 March 1960

Always stop! Always welcome!

Speeding by
go the buses
without stopping,
signalling
what I must never signal:
FULL . . .

12 May 1960

A four-handed piano?
I dream of much more:
music for a million hands,
harmony with the whole world joining in.

17 December 1961

A warning to the prosperous

It is not easy
to preserve
the soul of a jeep
in a Cadillac body.

2 January 1962

Some people are like sugar-cane:
even when crushed in the mill,
completely squashed,
reduced to pulp,
all they can yield is sweetness.

2 January 1962

At the insurance office
I got extremely interested
in the insuring of hands.

What value should be put on
the hands of artists?
the hands of doctors and nurses?
the hands of athletes?
the hands of writers?

What, oh, what value should be put
on hands that beg for alms, or give,
on hands that pray,
on hands that raise You, Lord?

3 January 1962

Looking at the goats
with chains round their necks
to stop them getting out of their pen
and invading the plantation,
I found the image I was seeking
for the excluded, under-developed world.

21 January 1962

I pray incessantly
for the conversion
of the prodigal son's
brother.

Ever in my ear
rings the dread warning:
'The one has awoken
from his life of sin.
When will the other
awaken
from his virtue?'

29 August 1962

When you are present to see
the scaffolding removed,
admire
—that's plain—
the building that emerges.
But ask after the scaffolding,
for it's no joke
to have served as support during construction,
to have been essential to the work
and then, on topping-out day,
to be removed
like rubbish.

29 August 1962

Gruesome definitions

Promiscuity:
intimacy without love.
Despair:
total absence
of anyone or anything
to cling to.
Utter loneliness:
living among the indifferent.
The cruellest yearning:
for those who are still with us.

30 August 1962

Do people weigh you down?

Don't carry them on your shoulders.
Take them into your heart.

30 August 1962

Don't let yourself be torn
between yesterday
and tomorrow.
Live always and only
God's today.

14 February 1964

Were You not to grant me the grace,
during the night-watches,
of drinking the silence,
of diving into it,
of being soaked in it,
how should I know
that inner silence,
without which
one can hear
neither man
nor You, Lord?

24 February 1964

Among the things to take with me,
I shall not forget you, Alarm-clock,
friend fixing the time for my vigils.

Without these,
Din City
would have devoured me.
The child inside me would have died,
having forgotten how to play
and overcome with fear.

Without them,
there would not be
this absolute trust
sealed forever
between us.

27 February 1964

If you want a dialogue,
don't insist on always
having the last word.
Behave as part . . .

28 February 1964

Of barriers to be broken down,
the hardest,
most important one
is undoubtedly
mediocrity.

8 March 1964

Put your ear to the ground
and identify the noises round you.
Predominant are
anxious, restless footsteps,
frightened footsteps in the dark,
footsteps bitter and rebellious.
No sound as yet
of hope's first footsteps.
Glue your ear to the ground again.
Hold your breath.
Put out your advance antennae:
The Master is on his way.
Most likely he will not get here
when things are going well,
but in bad times
when the going's unsure and painful.

21 April 1964

You have learnt life's lesson?

By this, you mean to say
that you've dried up inside
and insulate yourself
against the spontaneity
you now regret;
that you are prudent now,
with that bad prudence
implying lack of warmth,
quenching the sacred flame?

If so, I beg you,
live your whole life long
learning nothing from experience,
guileless with man,
childlike with God.

23 August 1966

They want to mend my pavement

I hadn't even noticed
it was broken.
I like
the humble little weed
which has sprouted there.
How can I make them understand
that it is far more lovely,
more alive,
than the cold cement
my friends want me to have?
If cement wins the day,
it will be a tombstone
invisibly inscribed:
'Here lies
the liveliest,
most tenacious,
cleverest little weed
for miles around.'

20 June 1969

Don't get annoyed
if the person coming to see you,
if the person wanting to talk to you,
can't manage to express
the uproar raging inside him.

Much more important
than listening to the words
is imagining the agonies,
fathoming the mystery,
listening to the silences . . .

9 July 1969

Total darkness

The night was so dark,
not the least speck of light,
so dark
that I was seized with panic
in spite of the deep love
I have always felt for night.

Then she told me her secret:
The darker the night is,
the lovelier usually is
the dawn she carries in her womb.

14 June 1970

The noise
that prevents us hearing
the voice of God
is not,
is truly not,
the clamour of man,
the racket of cities,
still less
the stirring of the wind
or the whispering of water.

The noise
that completely smothers
the voice of God
is the inner uproar
of outraged self-esteem,
of awakening suspicion,
of unsleeping ambition.

31 July 1970

The Offertory
—going on all day long—
lays before You
what my eyes see,
what my ears hear,
what my imagination guesses.
No paten . . .?
But haven't I my two hands?
No hosts . . .?
What about the unseen offerings
that eyes and ears,
imagination and the heart
incessantly take in?
And we ourselves,
aren't we
the integrating factor
in the Offertory?
No wine . . .?
Into the chalice
why not pour a drop
of the huge suffering
of men, my brothers?

The Consecration
—going on all day long—
reminds me
how alive and holy
is what issues from your hands.
Everything!
And I look round me, happy
to discover so much beauty
and to take my part in praising
everything occupying your divine mind
and sharing in your life
and in your holiness.
Alive and holy
the stars I gaze at from afar,
but also
the earth I tread,
the air I breathe,
the light enfolding me!
I draw no distinction
between what comes directly from You
and what is given to us
through the intermediacy of man,
the co-creator.

6 September 1970

The Communion
—going on all day long—
puts me
in deep and intimate contact
with all human creatures.
I laugh at barriers
of language, race, creed,
ideology.
Communion
makes me one
with all creation.
I am a citizen of Mars and Saturn,
linked
to all the stars,
to all the seas,
to every stone,
to every plant,
to all the animals.
To the spaces
and the voids,
to light and shadow,
to noise and silence,
to virtue and sin!
Limitlessly!

Without restriction!
I go where You go,
urgently to conquer the multiple
and incorporate it into the One.

6 September 1970

Universal consecration

Everything is touched with mystery
since everything comes
from your hands
or from those of the co-creator:
the paper on which I write,
the pen I use,
the table where I sit,
the books surrounding me,
the clothes I wear,
the air I breathe,
the light I gaze at,
the soil that bears me.
My heart thrills with joy,
a radiant sense
of universal unity.

24 April 1971

If I could,
I'd give every child
a terrestrial globe . . .
If possible, even
a globe that would light up,
in the hope
of opening those young eyes
as wide as they will go
and of arousing interest in,
and love for,
all peoples,
all races,
all tongues,
all religions!

27 June 1971

Accept
surprises
that upset your plans,
shatter your dreams,
give a completely
different turn
to your day
and—who knows?—
to your life.
It is not chance.
Leave the Father free
himself to weave
the pattern of your days.

6 July 1971

Let me not be the door
for going to my neighbour,
for bringing him to me
and forcing him
to walk along my paths,
to make my way-in his
and have to use my keys.
If my door is Christ,
what matters is
that I should help each brother
to travel to the Father
and yet still be himself.

8 July 1971

Don't cry
for rhythms
that seem to get lost:
the rhythms of the winds,
of the waters,
of the swaying of the trees,
of the singing of the birds,
of the motions of the stars,
of the footsteps of mankind.
There is always a musician
or a poet
or some saint
or someone deaf
whom God makes responsible
for catching
the wandering rhythms
before they get lost.

28 July 1971

An excellent thing it is
that your hand should assist take-off,
but may it never make so bold
as to take itself for the wings.

20 August 1971

Who can boast of being free?

Who has not got
secret prisons,
invisible chains,
all the more constricting
the less they are apparent?

5 September 1971

This puffy,
dirty face,
stained with sweat,
bruised by falls
or blows,
belongs to some beggar or drunkard?
Or are we perhaps on Calvary
gazing at the holy face
of the Son of God . . .?

19 September 1971

If you share your bread
in fear,
mistrustfully,
undaringly,
in a trice
your bread
will fail.
Try sharing it
without looking ahead,
not thinking of the cost,
unstintingly,
like a son of the Lord
of all the harvests in the world.

26 September 1971

Child, dearest child,
help me to wake
the child asleep
deep down deep
in the most sober-sided,
the most austere of men!

8 October 1971

Seeing the ink-stain on my coat
I thought of the invisible stains
made on us and those we make
not meaning to or noticing
throughout the day.

10 October 1971

Feel sorry, Lord,
have a special place in your heart
for those very logical,
practical,
rational people
who find it irritating
that other people believe
in the little blue horse!

11 October 1971

Is it true, Lord, that even today
You love the sight of water,
wind
and light?
Is it a fact that You are still affected
by birds,
by flowers,
by children?
What I am sure of is
that You love, just as much,
to see
what keeps emerging
from the hands of men
with whom You have shared
your creative power.

31 October 1971

If you have a thousand reasons for living,

If you never feel alone,
if you wake up wanting to sing,
if everything speaks to you,
from the stone in the road
to the star in the sky,
from the loitering lizard
to the fish, lord of the sea,
if you understand the winds
and listen to the silence,
rejoice,
for love walks with you,
he is your comrade,
is your brother!

28 January 1973

Teach us
to make our Noes
still have a smack of Yes
and never to say Yesses
that have a smack of No.

24 March 1973

Not even You,
with your irresistible look
of infinite goodness,
succeeded in moving
the heart
of the rich young man.
And yet he, from his childhood,
had kept
all the commandments.
Lord, my Lord, may we never,
out of mistaken charity,
water down
the terrible truths
You have spoken to the rich.

14 October 1973

Do you know why you never stop?

You think, perhaps,
it's a sense of responsibility,
a lack of time to waste,
distaste and scorn
for everything preventing you
from making the best use
of life's brief span.
The simple fact is this:
you are deceiving yourself
and trying to avoid
a self-to-self encounter.

4 August 1974

Why fear the dark?
How can we help but love it
when it is the darkness
that brings the stars to us?
What's more, who does not know
that on the darkest nights
is when the stars acquire
their greatest splendour?

8 October 1974

As long as the light lasts
the going will be easy . . .
Once the light fails
remember
that you can turn yourself
into a blazing torch
able to light up
pitch-black paths
and the most tortuous mazes.

14 February 1976

Why are you smiling, boy?

How happy I should feel
if that smile were to spring
from hope and self-assurance
as you face up to life!
I should feel happier still
if you could always learn
to keep that smile
of joy
when faced with goodness,
of sympathy
when faced with weakness,
of courage
when faced with failure,
of gratitude
when thinking about God!

14 February 1976

What a curious charm
autumn has
for me!
Why do I feel so happy
as the leaves
turn golden
or red,
when I know
they will soon be falling,
leaving the tree
stripped and bare?
My joy lies in the certainty
that life will prevail over death:
new buds will burst,
new leaves,
new fruit.

29 February 1976

Prudence, you have been so disfigured
that, to counterbalance
the weight of conformism,
compromise
and fear,
I almost feel the need
to shout,
'Be rash!'
Above all, don't forget
that boldness is a virtue,
more than a virtue,
a gift
of the Spirit of God.

29 February 1976

It is worth any sacrifice,
however great or costly,
to see eyes that were listless
light up again;
to see someone smile
who seemed to have forgotten
how to smile;
to see trust reborn
in someone
who no longer believed
in anything
or Anyone.

18 December 1976

112

Am I mistaken, Lord,
is it a temptation to think
You increasingly urge me
to go forth and proclaim
the need and urgency
of passing
from the Blessed Sacrament
to your other presence,
just as real,
in the Eucharist of the poor?
Theologians will argue,
a thousand distinctions be advanced . . .
But woe to him who feeds on You
and later has no eyes to see You,
to discern You
foraging for food among the garbage,
being evicted every other minute,
living in sub-human conditions
under the sign
of utter insecurity!

10 July 1977

At least at night
let your heart
have a rest . . .
At least at night
stop your career,
calm those desires
that nearly madden you,
see if you can manage
to put your dreams to sleep.
Yield yourself,
body and soul,
yield yourself
really,
truly and completely
into God's hands!

31 July 1977

There's no point
in going out of your way
to look for suffering,
to invent sacrifices,
to wear hair-shirts,
if you aren't willing
to embrace
the cross
which the Father has judged
to be
the right one for you.
Never forget:
this was no ready-made one.
The Father made it to measure
for your shoulders.

4 September 1977

The foreign geologist
irritably asked,
'Whenever will your country
become properly aware
of the immense wealth
hidden beneath its soil?'
This brought me up short,
appalled at the thought
of an incomparably graver
unawareness:
Whenever shall we human creatures
become properly aware
that we have,
hidden in our deepest selves,
the Lord of wealth,
and that he is being smothered
under incredible layers
of fatuous silliness,
absurd pretentiousness
and childish pride?

7 February 1978

Watching a marvellous film
about the ocean depths
I felt a huge desire
to help the fish
understand how lucky they are
to live immersed
in so much splendour.
Imagine then my thirst
to cry to men, my brothers,
that we live immersed—
coming and going,
swimming to and fro—
not in the oceans
but in God himself!

8 February 1978

The child had left
his toy-telephone
behind in our house.
I took the liberty of using it
before taking it back.
Here's a fine mystery!
Calls I had never managed to make,
so easily done,
so clear,
no interference,
on this instrument
wired with innocence
and love . . .

22 February 1978